The Actor's Machine

David Ihrig

Acknowledgements

Thank you to all the teachers that came before me, especially Gene Terruso and Kathryn Gately. Thanks to Jenny Graham, Anna Rubin, Scott Kudia and all the other teachers that taught alongside me, those I have met and the thousands I have not. And thanks to those actors who out of noble obligation to their audiences, are driven to be the best they can be. Turns out there are a bunch of us that actually do make "Much Ado" about . . . *something*.

CONTENTS

The Ihrig Approach

IS THERE A BETTER WAY?

"Everything happens to everybody sooner or later if there is time enough."

- Playwright, George Bernard Shaw

"We have not the time to take our time."

- Playwright, Eugene Ionesco

At some point, you *will* be called in for an audition that has the potential to change your life.

Make sure you are ready!

I've never met an actor who failed to work professionally, only those that gave up. Keep at it. Be good at what you do, and you will experience success.

Yet, every actor should realize the immediacy of his or her predicament. When it comes to developing our acting skills, "We have not the time to take our time."

We need to be ready now!

Time is also our most valuable resource during the discovery and rehearsal process. Professional stage productions schedule only three weeks of rehearsal for a full-length play. Cinematic productions typically meet for one rehearsal—or none at all.

If you want to work consistently as an actor, you need to show directors and producers you can produce results in the allotted time period. Directors want good actors, they want talented actors, but most of all they want actors that can deliver every time without fail. In fact, being an actor who can deliver is half the battle.

For all these reasons, *efficient* training and an *efficient* creative process are imperative to your success as an actor. You simply do not have time to waste.

The question we should all ask is:

> What can we do to be the best we can be as fast as possible?

Conventional wisdom tells us there is no shortcut. Most say it takes decades to become a master actor. But innovations can make conventional wisdom outdated.

The vast majority of actor's training is *effective,* but not *efficient.*

The inefficiency is caused by the uncertainty of what exactly constitutes the foundational skills of acting.

To master any skill, you must first have a solid foundation. And building on a proper foundation allows the rest of your training to happen much more efficiently, aka faster.

The purpose of this book is to provide that foundation.

In 1994, I lived in Chicago. At that time, Chicago produced more theater than any other city in the world, save New York City. To this day there is no established theater district in Chicago, but virtually every neighborhood in the city has storefront and warehouse spaces that serve as a theater. There were multiple shows opening every weekend.

I had just left grad school and was working with a theater company I suspect is now defunct. The company's name was Theater Q, and consisted of a small group of dedicated actors, writers and directors who sought to provide a safe place for artists to grow and experiment. Their mission statement was so inclusive that even a blond- haired blue-eyed frat-boy jock from New Jersey (that was me) felt at home. At meetings I would look around the room and see people that were so different from one another, and yet in some ways we were all the same.

The company was producing a series of table-readings at a local bookstore. A table-reading is a performance where actors stay seated at a table with the scripts in their hands and act out a play. The evening's performance consisted of three ten-minute original plays, and the company's manager invited me to direct one of the pieces. I was grateful for the opportunity. I wanted to try something new, so I asked permission to use a non-traditional casting and rehearsal process. It was granted.

I had a theory. I wanted to see if an entire performance could be created around the performer's ability to listen. I was formally trained in the Meisner technique, which is an actor's training technique consisting primarily of improvisational exercises designed specifically to teach an actor to listen and respond. As a result of developing our listening skills, I'd seen some incredible transformations take place in my university classmates and in myself.

I wondered if there wasn't a way to rehearse a play by focusing the actor's entire discovery process on their listening skills. If it didn't work I could always abandon the idea halfway in rehearsal and use a traditional process. After all, it was a table-reading and the actors would have the script in their hands anyway.

At the auditions, I brought in two actors at a time and asked each actor to perform their monologue with the other actor. The actor without lines was instructed to listen. Although they were likely unaware of it, the listening actor was actually the one being auditioned.

The assistant director and I easily agreed on the three actors that were the best listeners.

We had only one week and three rehearsals before the performance. At the first rehearsal, I dropped the bomb on the cast—they would not receive the script. Instead, they would each receive a list of *objective* information about their character and the play. Based on that information, they would improvise each scene. During the scene improvisations, they would receive only two directions from me. I would either call out "repeat" or "observe." When I said "repeat," they had to literally repeat the words the other actor had just said. When I said "observe," the actor had to make a verbal observation about the other character.

If you think this sounds a bit wacky, I don't blame you. I really hadn't thought it all the way through. And frankly, I didn't know if the actors would get anything of value from the experiment or if I was just wasting everyone's time.

But there was no turning back now. We were all assembled at rehearsal.

Naturally, my assistant and I were very familiar with the script. But the actors knew only the objective information that we fed them. They knew they were sisters. They knew the single sister was visiting the married pregnant sister's home. We shared only the facts that were presented in the script. We purposely shared nothing subjective—no personality traits, no feelings, no judgments.

During the improvisations, when it appeared to me the actors didn't understand what was happening between them, I would simply say "repeat" until the two actors established a truthful communication.

For example, when the single sister came to the door, the pregnant sister welcomed her with a hug and said, "Hi!"

The single sister stood in the doorway for a moment. I said, "Repeat!"

The single sister said, "Hi."

She was a bit uneasy. I told the pregnant sister to "observe."

The pregnant sister said, "You look uncomfortable." This was the scene's first moment.

The way the process evolved, I would tell them to repeat again and again until they found the behavior(s) the scene demanded. And once they discovered them organically through their interactions, I would tell them to observe so they would recognize and internally label those moments as meaningful.

Using only this process, I was loosely guiding the improvised scene to mirror the playwright's storyline.

And then something wonderful happened.

One of the actors actually spoke a line from the play!

My assistant and I turned our heads simultaneously to discover each other's jaws had dropped. During our first rehearsal, an actor organically discovered the words of the playwright without ever having seen the script.

Moreover, using the repeat/observe process to guide them, these two actors organically discovered the themes of the play, which revolved around the single sister's jealously of her sibling and her feelings of inadequacy because she had not yet settled down.

But the best part of this story is yet to come.

The night before the performance, our third rehearsal, was the first time the actors actually set eyes on the script. We read it at the table a few times, and it was the most solid first reading of a script I'd ever witnessed.

The cast asked if we could stage it. They didn't want to do it as a table-reading; they wanted to add movement to the piece. They contended they "knew it too well" to stay at the table. They had been rehearsing the play with movement and it felt *unnatural* to stay seated at a table.

They convinced me, so we decided to block the show.

Blocking is typically determined by the director, who chooses the actor's positions or movement on stage for each scene. However, in this process, the actors had already *organically* discovered their movement. We made only a few minor adjustments to accommodate for the entrances and exits during scene changes, but otherwise the movements were already set.

After a few effortless run-throughs, the cast had yet another request. They unanimously asked to perform the piece off-book, meaning without the script. I thanked them for their enthusiasm and willingness to expend the energy to memorize ten pages of dialogue in one night, but I told them it wasn't really necessary.

All three actors persisted. They felt like they were nearly off-book already.

I was dumbfounded. This was the very first time they had seen the script! With only three rehearsals, all three actors felt so comfortable in their roles they were ready to mount a full production the next day!

And that's what happened.

The performance was a success, and the audience/actor discussion afterward was lively.

Before we all get carried away, I need to be clear—this book is not about the repeat/observe process. The fact that it *worked* is not nearly as important as *how* and *why* it worked. The process was simply the structure that allowed us to explore the creative process from a different perspective.

It is that perspective that holds the key to mastery.

The goal of this book is to capture and implement the *unconscious discovery process* that occurred within each of those actors.

In the following pages you will discover for yourself the perspective that allowed them to "know the play" so well in such a short amount of time.

This book is written so you can develop the perspective and strategies of a master actor. It's about identifying and clearly labeling the successful underlying principles of that experiment in order to provide the actor with an efficient and effective set of tools.

At the time of this experiment, I had little knowledge of human behavior. I've since embarked on a quest to understand human nature at a level that would allow me to improve the way I teach. I've become a certified practitioner of Neuro-Linguistic Programming and discovered that the fields of psychology, linguistics, human development and behavior all hold rich and valuable information for the actor. And for the past twenty years, I've been working with actors to develop, organize and hone the ideas and techniques you will find outlined in this book.

The Ihrig Approach offers a fresh perspective for the actor.

It gives actors something they won't get anywhere else— an understanding of the actor's tool, a blueprint to how humans process information and produce behavior naturally. You'll learn how to incorporate this information into your own acting technique.

In short, I believe this book lays out the most direct path available today to master the craft of acting.

I wish you a wonderful and shortened journey.

The Ihrig Approach

Great acting performances are *unconscious*.

By this I mean an actor cannot be consciously aware of his or her behaviors during performance. In great performances, *behaviors* occur naturally, just like in real life.

Great performances allow the audience to believe they are witnessing real life. Therefore, the actor's goal should be to create real life behavior.

What is real life behavior? Webster's defines *behavior* as "Anything that an organism does involving action and response to stimulation." An actor "responding to stimulation" in the same way as in real life is the foundation of great acting. We will explore this idea in great detail throughout this book. But first, the most important thing to realize about human behavior is that it is a largely unconscious process. We do not consciously decide to laugh when something strikes us as humorous. The laugh is an unplanned behavior, a spontaneous response which happens outside of our awareness, also known as *unconsciously.*

The actor's behavior is the most important aspect of storytelling. If you distill the audience's experience of great acting down to its final form, the end result is authentic behavior.

Think about this for a moment.

It doesn't matter whether the story is told on film or stage. The curtain rises, or the camera pans, and the audience is introduced to a setting. The opening images stimulate the audience for just a short while. The audience doesn't become engaged in the story until the viewer identifies the main character and sees him or her interact with their world. How the main character interacts with the world is observed through his or her behavior. The character's *behavior* allows the audience to take away meaning.

In any story told with actors, hereby referred to as dramatic storytelling, behavior is the key element.

Yet, despite the importance of behavior, few actors have been formally exposed to a working knowledge of their own unconscious behavior-producing processes. Until now, there has been no widespread actor's training that provides the actor with scientifically supported information about human behavior.

This book will give the artist a tangible understanding of his or her own behavior-producing machinery. The approach will give you a new perspective when tackling the greatest question you face as an actor:

How do you "live truthfully in imaginary circumstances?"

Constantine Stanislavski (1863–1938), the father of modern acting, was amongst the first to ask that question and propose an answer. He believed that "living truthfully" was an unconscious process. The last chapter of his famous book, An Actor Prepares, (1980 p. 245) is titled, *On the Threshold of the Subconscious*. In the second paragraph he states, "The fundamental objective of our psycho-technique is to put us in a creative state in which our subconscious will function naturally."

The entire book describes how an actor 'prepares consciously in order to perform unconsciously.' Unconscious performance has largely been the unspoken goal of actors since the beginning.

So, how did this Stanislavski fellow and his technique become so widespread?

In case you're not familiar with him, Constantine Stanislavski was a Russian theater director and actor who decided his stories would be better told on stage in a realistic style. He decided to create a theater in which actors stopped pretending or "representing behaviors," and instead experienced realistic behaviors that could be observed by the audience.

Realistic acting has been the standard ever since.

As such, virtually every acting technique taught in America today stems from Stanislavski's work. Stella Adler, Sandy Meisner, Lee Strasberg, and Michael Chekhov, all of America's most prominent acting teachers, studied with Stanislavski and brought his work back to America. Here his teachings became the foundation for all realistic acting techniques, most notably The Method.

If we look at the theatrical devices and styles that existed before Stanislavski, there is evidence of actors experiencing real emotion on stage, but no documented widespread attempt at realism as we know it today. Actors were trained in stock stances and expressions that *represented* emotions. Most of us are aware that in Shakespearean theater, young boys played the female roles. Historic paintings often depict makeup and masks that are caricature-like. And most of the pre-realism scripts were set in exotic lands and written about kings and royalty. Many scripts were written in verse, much like a rhyming poem.

Stanislavski was developing his system during the same time period when emerging realistic playwrights such as Henrik Ibsen and Anton Checkov were experimenting with their craft. Their new plays focused on middle class problems set in middle class settings, and attempted to capture the psychological struggles of the common man. The combination of new literary content and the new style of acting had as large an impact on the art form as any single innovation. Imagine how the audience reacted the first time they watched it.

Theatergoers apparently liked it quite a bit, because realism spread like wildfire. Russian theater expert

Constantin Rudinsky described Stanislavski's production of Checkov's play *The Seagull* as "one of the greatest new developments in the history of world drama."

Stanislavski had to tackle a whole new set of problems—he had to train his actors to do something new. So he set about to study how people talked and behaved in real life. He had to figure out how to teach his actors to behave naturally while playing a character created by the imagination of a playwright.

Stanislavski studied everything that was available to him at the time, including Darwinism, Yoga, Pavlovian behavioral psychology, psychophysiology, and a multitude of philosophies.

In the 1930s, a delegation of American actors traveled to Russia to study at the Moscow Art Theater. This party of young actors were members of the Group Theater. Their goal was to learn from the master himself and to bring back his teachings to the New York City theater scene. From The Group Theater emerged America's important acting teachers. Among them were Stella Adler, Lee Strasberg, and Sandy Meisner.

There is a well-known dispute in the interpretation of Stanislavki's teaching about how an actor should work with emotions. While members of the group were studying at the Moscow Art Theater, Stanislavski was teaching Emotional Recall, a technique where actors recall emotional situations from their own lives just before performing so that they enter the performance in an emotional state. Emotional Recall was adopted by the group and brought back to America. But Stanislavski later decided that Emotional Recall wasn't the right way to go. He believed an actor would be limited by his own life experiences and presumably unable to create the necessary full range of emotions required. In other words, this tenacious, hard-working, and dedicated man was not *satisfied* with his work. He was probably never really satisfied.

Consider that all of his teachings are predicated upon the most up-to-date information that was available to him at the time. Because he died in 1938, it's safe to say that there is information available to us today that was not available to Stanislavski in his lifetime. Yet, for the most part, we still teach actors largely based upon the principles, if not the exact teachings, of his method.

Why?

Because, it works. As do most of the variations and derivatives of Stanislavski's actor's training methods taught in today's acting schools.

I myself received my training in the Meisner technique. Sandy Meisner was one of the members of The Group Theater that went to study with Stanislavski. He subsequently created his famous repetition exercises designed to teach actors how to "live truthfully *moment to moment* in imaginary circumstances." Sandy added the phrase "moment to moment" to Stanislavski's definition because he believed that "being present" in the moment was the key to achieving great performances.

I studied the Meisner technique for two years as an undergraduate, decided I'd like to teach, and went to a graduate program that focused on the technique. I completed my training, received my degree, and began to teach.

But at some point after graduate school, a thought occurred to me.

If the actor's job is to "live truthfully in imaginary circumstances," shouldn't I know something about how *I* live truthfully in non-imaginary circumstances? That thought consumed and inspired me.

This book is a direct result of that question.

To find that answer, I began reading everything I believed would give me a better understanding of the human mind and behavior. And I found some really useful stuff, which I couldn't wait to pass on to my students. And what I found was, when I armed my students with information about how they lived truthfully in non-imaginary circumstances, aka real life, the actor's training learning curve was significantly shortened.

It was cut in half!

The current offerings of knowledge from the fields of psychology, linguistics, physiology, neurology, etc., are rich with nuggets that are immensely helpful for actors. Much of the mystery about how our minds work has been removed since Stanislavski created his technique. Although not well known, there are very useful, concrete practices available to actors today.

So let's get back to Stanislavski who was ahead of *his* time but not of ours. He said, "In order to perform unconsciously, actors prepare consciously."

This works.

But what if there was a way to make it work better? What if there was a way to "prepare *unc*onsciously in order to perform unconsciously?"

Now that would be something, wouldn't it?

Stanislavski repeatedly told his actors, "Create your own method. Don't depend slavishly on mine. Make up something that will work for you! But keep breaking traditions, I beg you."

Maybe it was he who whispered in my ear all those years ago, "How *do* we live in real life circumstances?"

KEY POINTS

1. Stanislavski believed that great acting performances are unconscious.

2. Contemporary actor's training is based on scientific knowledge from the 1900s.

Chapter 2

JOB TRAINING

What are actors trying to do?

We've all heard the old adage, "if you don't know where you're going, how will you ever get there?"

Let's start with the actor's purpose.

Without actors, there is no dramatic storytelling form. And story, my friends, is undoubtedly the most powerful and influential force to shape humanity.

Stories are the primary movers of most of humanity's beliefs. The stories of Jesus, Muhammad, Buddha, have been told for thousands of years and have created the societies we live in. Story is how humans process information and assign meaning to events. Story is how we make sense of life. Storytelling is the most effective communication tool in the history of mankind.

Robert McKee, in the quintessential screenwriting book entitled *Story* (1997, p.113) says, "Storytelling is the creative demonstration of truth." And the actor is the demonstrator. The actor dramatizes a story and brings it to life in front of an audience's eyes. If done well, the experience is cathartic.

Great acting requires skills most people aren't even aware of. The average person has no idea what happens in an acting class. They have no idea how much time, effort, and sacrifice it takes to become an actor. And if they happen to know an actor and witness the life choices of a dramatic artist, they can't for the life of them figure out why anyone would do it.

I think many of us become actors because at our core we understand the importance of the job. The President of the United States, bigwig CEO's, professionals—none of them truly have the ability to affect their fellow human beings the way dramatic artists do. Because as actors, aka the great "Demonstrators of Truth," we effect change in an audience from the inside, communicating to a person on many levels. We allow them to make sense of their world in a personal and intimate way that transcends all other forms of communication. An audience member engaged in a well-told dramatized story literally leaves a performance a different person than when they arrived. Actors, with the help of our story-telling teams (writers, directors, etc.), affect untold numbers of people without ever setting eyes on them.

That's the power of great story telling.

So how do we learn to be a master "truth demonstrator?"

Many new actors say they need to learn how to "memorize the lines," or "learn facial expressions." Actors have asked me to teach them to "cry on stage," or to be able to create other real emotions. Typically, actors will recognize at some point in their progression the need to learn to *listen* onstage.

More experienced actors will express a desire to *just be*, or to *live in the moment*. Popular phrases are "to immerse oneself in the role," "become the character" and "to live truthfully."

All of these aspirations have a degree of importance and value.

Some of them can be taught in a tangible manner. If you want to learn to memorize your lines, there are simple, easy steps to follow. But, though memorizing your lines is a necessary step, being the best memorizer in the history of the world won't make one a great actor. Neither does any single isolated skill an actor works to learn.

And what about the loftier goals of learning to *be the character*, or *live truthfully*? How does an actor achieve those things?

Reaching those goals rarely happens quickly, and frankly, for most it never happens at all. Actors who master their craft do so through years of hard work and dedication to their art.

As an acting teacher, if I say to a beginning actor, "Do that scene again, but this time live truthfully," what do they do? If simply giving the instruction, "live truthfully" worked, we would be surrounded by master actors. But we're not. Because whether you're trained formally or informally in one particular technique or another, we must all learn through experience. We must learn by good old-fashioned trial and error. What works for one actor does not necessarily work for another. And when we are given a task as ambiguous and broad as learning to "live truthfully," where is one to start?

The vastness of this task is the birth-child to many different actor's training methods and techniques. Most seek to break down the task of *living truthfully* into smaller components, or skill sets. There are acting exercises that isolate individual skill sets such as working emotionally, or listening, or exploring physicality, etc. There are classes that develop the actor's vocal instrument. And again, there is great value in learning all these skills.

And yet, mastery of any one of these components does not make one a master actor.

Acting is not like throwing a shot put. You don't get to measure your results in something as definitive and clear cut as feet and inches.

Most actors don't have a clear goal in mind when it comes to mastering their craft. They may have desires, but they don't have a definitive goal with tangible action steps. They must rely on a teacher to define their destination and then map their route.

In my experience, I have found many actors don't even have a clear understanding of the actor's job. So before you set a goal for yourself, let's start by clearly defining the actor's job.

The Actor's Job

The actor's job is to perform a role in a believable way so that the audience can lose themselves in a story.

Actors are the visible members of the team that tells a story. The writer imagines and then represents the story using words. The director chooses the frame through which the story will be experienced. The designers and crew bring that frame into existence. And the actor lives through a few carefully chosen moments of the characters' lives.

As long as the actor doesn't do anything to jolt the viewer from their unconscious state of story-watching, she has done her job. The moment she pulls the audience out of the story, she has failed.

And what will pull the audience out of the story?

Bad acting.

Think about the words that describe bad acting: wooden, stiff, over the top, fake. These words describe opposite ends in the spectrum of bad acting. But either way, what we really mean to say is the *character's behavior does not fit the context of the situation or story.*

Bad acting is conscious, forced, contrived human behavior. In my opinion, it most often happens because of the conscious awareness of the act of acting itself.

You can't get away with faking real behavior for an audience.

23

Why?

Because every single one of us is an expert in human behavior! As babies, we were fixated on our parent's faces. We have studied facial expressions our entire lives. Before we could speak, we learned to recognize and comprehend human behavior in order to communicate our needs. Our survival depended upon it.

What is it exactly do audiences observe and subsequently label as bad acting? And more importantly, and the point of this book, what is it that audiences observe and label great acting?

In great acting, audiences observe *behavior* that is contextually accurate. The understanding that behavior happens as a result of context, or circumstances, is an extremely important one. The result of living truthfully in imaginary circumstances is *authentic behavior*.

Webster's defines authentic as "worthy of acceptance or belief as conforming to fact or reality. Not imaginary, false or imitation." Semantically, actors get into trouble with the word truthful, especially early in their training when they tend to mistakenly label behavior they don't yet understand as untruthful. Calling a behavior *authentic*, or "conforming to reality," is contextually accurate.

Thus, the actor's job is to create *authentic behavior*.

To grasp the importance and scope of authentic behavior, let's go to an expert outside of our field.

Gavin Debecker is a security expert, and has long been fascinated with the behaviors of both criminals and victims. In his book *Gift of Fear* (1997), he suggests that intuition is the gut response to unconscious observations that don't add up. He says victims of crimes very often report an uneasy feeling immediately before being victimized.

Here's an example of a real life story from DeBecker's book.

A young woman enters her apartment building and is startled when a stranger suddenly appears outside her door. The stranger is smiling, apologizes for startling her and offers to help her with her bags. Feeling that something isn't right, she at first refuses.

DeBecker astutely points out that the young woman's "gut instinct" is the result of a series of unconscious observations of things she *should* have heard based on her past experience. Things such as *not* having heard the door open or close after she entered the building. She also didn't hear the sound of the man's footsteps. Her unconscious mind "remembered" the patterns of stimulus (the sounds of footsteps, etc.) that did *not* occur in order for a person to be outside her door. In reality, the man was hiding in the hallway waiting for her to arrive.

Consider that process. The stimulus of the man showing up immediately triggered a retrospective assessment to determine what was missing from the patterns her mind had stored. It instantaneously set off a biochemical reaction to warn the system that something was awry. And that response was entirely outside of the woman's conscious awareness.

This incredible feat performed by our minds is only a sliver of the capabilities of the incredible machine we inhabit. And this incredible machine is the tool of the artist known as the actor. I offer a more complete understanding of our machines so actors can substantially accelerate the growth of their skill set.

Think of the complexity of human behavior. We respond to things of which we are not consciously aware. There is depth and complexity to every waking moment. This can't be replicated consciously. It can't be faked.

Now, let's pretend we have to play the scene of the young woman who is surprised in the hallway. Try to *consciously* represent all the psychological and physiological steps that occur in the single moment she notices the man. Choose *consciously* to move the seven facial muscles that raise your eyebrows as you draw a short breath. Simultaneously, hide the fact you are doing it, and then breathe out quickly. Now send adrenaline into your bloodstream, change the color in your face, throw in a fleeting micro expression as you remember the time you were embarrassed for being scared at age eight, quickly dilate your pupils… you get the picture.

You can't do it. Why not?

Because behavior is created *unconsciously.*

This is the great dilemma. How do we deliver a performance that engages our natural unconscious responses which are fully informed by the circumstances of the story?

Most accomplished actors say they must fully understand the circumstances of the story in order to allow the behavior to flow. And in order to fully understand the circumstances, you must research. You must read the script. Most great actors read everything they can about the world of the story. They research the time period, the culture, and the character's profession, everything they can find.

But here again is an interesting dilemma for the actor.

Reading is a 'left brain' process. Left brain is a term that describes thought processes that are linear and analytical. The mechanisms that process that type of information are believed to take place mostly in the left hemisphere of the brain. In fact, it is believed that virtually all language processing—the reading of the script, the verbal notes the director gives, the discussions you have about your character—all happens from the left side of your brain.

And guess where the mechanisms responsible for creativity, emotions, and behavior are believed to be located? If you guessed the right side, you are correct.

Actors have been working to assimilate information from the left brain by using the right brain ever since Stanislavski introduced the world to realistic acting. Whether it's a piece of dialogue the actor reads from a script, or a bit of information about religious beliefs in a specific time period, the challenge is the same.

How does the actor get a piece of important information "in" them?

Since the inception of realistic acting, each actor has had to discover his or her own way to effectively accomplish this task, totally unaware of the left brain vs. right brain dilemma. Traditionally, actors simply try different things until something works, and then do their best to replicate what felt right.

Is there a more efficient way to bridge the gap from the conscious processes actors must use to prepare for a role in order to achieve unconscious performance? Is there a more direct route?

Yes.

By using what we know today from the fields of psychology, neurosciences and behavioral sciences, we can significantly shorten the learning curve toward becoming a great actor.

You're about to learn a process that engages your natural unconscious systems. By working in this manner, you will bypass the majority of pitfalls created in a strictly left brained approach.

Your goal is to consistently create authentic behavior in performance. This may seem daunting and mysterious. But it's not.

The first step is to understand how behavior is created in real life. Using this knowledge, we can apply very simple concrete steps to create authentic behavior in the dramatic art form we know as acting.

In the next chapter, you will learn about the behavior-producing machine you inhabit. And then you will learn about the fuels the machine uses to produce behavior.

KEY POINTS

1. The actor's job is to create authentic behavior.

2. Authentic behavior is too complex to fake or create consciously.

3. Creating authentic behavior is a right brained process.

Chapter 3

LIVING TRUTHFULLY... IN REAL LIFE

Now that you have an understanding of authentic behavior and the job of the actor, you might begin to see how simple great acting *should* be.

Theoretically, contemporary realistic acting should be pretty easy. Don't we "behave authentically" every day when we're not on stage?

In contrast, remember actors throughout history had to learn representational acting, which meant they had to memorize physical stances and practice specific facial expressions before they could perform for their audiences. Realistic actors simply have to behave naturally, right?

However, realistic actors have to behave naturally in imaginary circumstances. So before we tackle the challenge of creating authentic behavior in imaginary circumstances, let's first learn how behavior is created in real life.

To do so, you will be introduced to two scientific theorems that are extremely important to the actor's process. Just as a competent racecar driver must know the basics of the mechanics of his engine, you too will understand the basics of your behavior-producing engine. The two simple concepts that will help you better understand your engine is:

1. The Actor's Blueprint

2. Pattern Completion in Human Learning

The Actor's Blueprint

What determines human behavior in any given moment?

How does your behavior-producing machine work?

Here's the blueprint.

Think of humans as behavior-producing machines.

Information is our fuel, and behavior is our product. Information is constantly flowing into us from the outside world. We see things. We hear things. We feel things. And that constant flow of information produces human behavior.

ACTOR'S BLUEPRINT

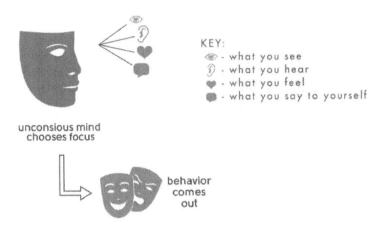

KEY:
- what you see
- what you hear
- what you feel
- what you say to yourself

unconsious mind
chooses focus

behavior
comes
out

The mind's natural processes constantly take in sensory information, sift through that information, categorize the stimulus for valence (importance), and then *respond* to the selected stimulus by either completing patterns of behavior learned from past experience, or working to identify and then store new patterns.

I suspect that 20% of you just glazed over the description above, 20% got excited, and 60% re-read it just to try and make sense of it. But all of you are wondering how it's going to help you become a great actor.

The first important thing for an actor to recognize is everything in the description above happens outside of your conscious awareness.

This book is about to introduce you to the most powerful part of you, and the place from whence all acting discoveries, processes, and performances should come.

Meet the engine of your behavior-producing machinery.

Meet your *unconscious mind*.

Most of us haven't really spent much time thinking about or getting to know our unconscious minds. There is sort of a stigma tied to the unconscious mind. Many people associate the inner workings of the mind with the work of the famous psychologist Sigmund Freud. And even though much of his work has been largely disproved, we still associate the unconscious mind with hidden traumas of childhood, suppressed sexual fantasies, and all kinds of embarrassing things unfit for social conversation. Or the term "unconscious mind" might conjure up images of hypnotists who coerce unsuspecting audience members to embarrass themselves in public. We just don't have many positive associations with the unconscious mind, and yet we now know:

Your unconscious mind is the most loving, protective, creative and truly miraculous part of you.

Why do I say that?

Do you have to remind yourself to breathe each night before you go to bed?

How much conscious effort goes into digesting your food?

Have you ever arrived somewhere and suddenly realized you don't remember the trip because you were daydreaming? Yet you arrived safe and sound.

Your unconscious mind does all this for you and more. It stores and recalls your memories. And it does all these things for you without calling on your conscious mind so that you can go about doing whatever you choose.

What is touching your skin right now? Before you read this, you probably didn't notice. Is it the chair against your backside? Is it the clothes you're wearing? A breeze? You probably aren't consciously aware of the background noise in your environment. How many mechanical noises are in your space right now? There may be the humming of a fan or appliance motor. There may be people talking nearby, or the sounds of birds. As you're reading this right now, think of all the other bits of visual information that are within your view, but you don't notice them until you move your focus.

Your unconscious mind took all the unnecessary information out of your awareness so that you could focus on reading and digesting these words.

How much information is being tossed around in your neurology right now?

Science tells us—a lot. We see, we hear, we smell, and we feel. And all of that sensory information is plugged in and communicated to our brains constantly through a network of neurological connections.

Picture your neurological connections as many different tiny interconnected pathways or wires going from all the places in your body that take in information: the skin of your fingertips, the photoreceptors in your eyes, the sound receptors in your ears, etc. Electrical impulses travel up and down these pathways to provide the processing centers of your brain with information. There are more neurological connections in your body than grains of sand on all the beaches in the world. That's a lot of connections.

If we were to attempt to process all the information coursing through our machine at any given moment, we would be paralyzed and probably go insane. Fortunately, our protector, the unconscious mind, pares down all this information for us to seven bits of information, plus or minus two, which allows us to manage that information.

Neuroscientists tell us all behavior happens at the unconscious level. In the previous chapter, we discussed the impossibility of consciously triggering the movements of hundreds of muscles and molecular chemical reactions that naturally occur when we experience an emotion. And for those actors who try to fake behavior, the audience easily recognizes that behavior as fake because it lacks the natural complexity of authentic behavior.

The father of modern drama, Constantin Stanislavski, has said from the very beginning of the realistic acting movement that "actors must prepare consciously in order to perform subconsciously." In his most famous book, *An Actor Prepares*, Stanislavski mentions the subconscious mind on virtually every page. Yet, to my knowledge, this approach is the only concrete exploration of how an actor can use their unconscious mind as a substantial and tangible part of their process.

Please take away this if nothing else: an actor cannot consciously force authentic behavior from his machinery.

However, an actor can consciously provide the fuel for his or her machinery to produce authentic behavior naturally.

Great acting, or the production of authentic behavior, happens when an actor consciously provides the right fuel or input to his or her behavior-producing machinery.

The scientific word for behavior-producing fuel is *stimulus*. Simply put, stimulus is the thing that you respond to at any given moment.

Actors simply need to know what specific stimulus to present to their unconscious minds in order to experience the natural behaviors appropriate to the circumstances of the story.

You're going to learn to identify different types of stimulus. You're going to learn how to choose the right stimulus. And then you're going to learn how to use stimulus to discover the experience of your character and to allow unconscious performances. But first, you need to understand another human behavior model called *pattern completion*.

Pattern Completion in Human Learning

Humans learn by completing patterns.

For actors, understanding and implementing the natural process of pattern completion can unlock the secret to delivering compelling and active performances. You will hear more about this in a subsequent chapter, but first let's explore pattern completion.

Pattern completion is how we learn. We categorize and store our experiences. This likely begins while we are still in the womb. From the very beginning, our mind works to identify patterns in order to predict outcomes.

We hear a sound, and based on our past experiences, if we recognize the sound as non-threatening or non-interesting, we ignore it. But if we don't recognize the sound, we take notice. Our circuitry is designed to respond. Remember, our neurology is constantly taking in information, and our unconscious mind decides what stimulus deserves a response.

Our responses are based on past experience, or the lack thereof.

A parent hears a child cry. Without thinking about it, the parent immediately determines if the sound came from their child and the nature of the cry. The parent may do nothing and wait for the cry to subside on its own, or dash to the rescue. What determines their response? The experienced parent is able to complete the pattern immediately. They know the variations of crying and have linked those tones to situations that needed immediate responses and those that didn't.

For example, at some time in the past, the parent heard an angry-toned cry and arrived to find that one child had taken a toy from the other. No emergency. Another time the parent heard a fearfully-toned cry and arrived to find that the child had fallen out of bed and was hurt. This needed immediate attention. Each respective cry and its outcome was stored for later use.

Inexperienced parents, on the other hand, jump to their feet every time their child cries. They haven't had enough experience to recognize the tone of the cry and to link it to an outcome. So they seek to learn the pattern by physically running to check on the child.

In both examples, the parent's unconscious mind is *actively completing patterns*.

Here's another example.

Imagine you hear a loud crash. When a human experiences something they don't normally experience, like a loud crash, our mechanisms stop to assess the information so that our next action ensures survival. As we've already discussed, we first determine if the sound matches sounds we've heard before. If not, we ask what made the sound? How far away is the sound? Is it far enough away that we can escape from the thing, or do we have to ready ourselves for defense? Of course I'm describing the well-known flight or fight response.

And there's that word again—*response.*

Let's recap "real life." All kinds of information comes into us through our eyes, ears, touch receptors, and internal feedback from our storage processes. Our unconscious mind picks out what's important to us, focuses on it so that our machine can identify and/or complete patterns from past experience. This triggers some sort of psychological/physiological response also known as *behavior.*

John Wayne's famous quote about acting, "I don't act, I re-act," sums up what most contemporary acting methods teach.

What if we apply our natural response processes from real life to our acting? What if we thought about the stimulus our characters were responding to? And possibly even what patterns our characters were completing or attempting to complete as a result of their past experience with the given stimulus?

Are you beginning to see how this process can be applied in performance?

Great acting happens when you discover what your character is responding to, and you focus on that stimulus to allow natural behavior to ensue.

It is interesting to note again that you *naturally* produce authentic behavior every day. When you think about acting in this way, you realize you naturally possess the skills of a great actor! You actually have to *work* to be a bad actor. You actually have to take steps to get in the way of a great performance. Most of us simply have to unlearn bad habits that we have come to know as acting, or stop ourselves from creating unnecessary habits.

Moving forward, you now have a solid foundation of the knowledge necessary to comprehend this approach, and we're getting close to applying this information to your craft.

This next idea is a true miracle that most of us take for granted. Remember that all of the necessary functions for survival are taken care of by our unconscious minds (breathing, digesting, etc.). Because of this, human beings get to choose their conscious focus in any given moment.

Napoleon Hill wrote a very famous book entitled *Think and Grow Rich* (1960). He outlines the principles of success he learned from interviews with some of the most successful people in the world. He states early in the book that the greatest gift a human has is the ability to control his thoughts.

The same principle that brought success in the form of financial windfalls is at your fingertips as an actor. We've been doing it for so long, we don't give it a second thought. But consider now—the thoughts we choose directly determine our outcomes.

And the thoughts we choose determine the meaning we derive in any given moment. Therefore, the thoughts we choose determine our behaviors.

A process we largely ignore is directly responsible for the outcomes in our lives, and most importantly, is directly responsible for our behavior.

The fact that we have the ability to control and direct our thoughts is why this approach works. Because we can choose our focus in a moment, we have the ability to craft our performances and deliver great acting. I can choose to look at a basketball and remember the time I missed the shot and lost the game, or choose another time when I made the shot and won the game. Each choice brings a different response and therefore a different behavior. I can also choose to ignore the basketball and notice the way my scene partner is covering his hand as if he's hiding something.

What I'd like my students to learn is how to discover the character's experience by "directing their focus" to the most important elements of the character's circumstances. Authentic behavior will then come naturally.

It is your *focus* in any given moment that determines your behavior.

Take a moment to look out the window. Notice your experience. What do you choose to focus on? A bird? A nice car? An old car? Children playing? A bush? Noises? Now turn your focus to a photograph you have. Turn your focus to the person next to you. If no one is there, notice how that feels. Think about someone you miss right now.

Now focus on the idea that you are on your way to consistently creating brilliant performances.

The actor's job is to first discover the specific stimulus in the *imaginary circumstances* that causes the appropriate behavior in a scene, then to place your focus on that stimulus and allow yourself to naturally respond to it.

Simply put, find the thing that causes your character to respond and allow yourself to respond to it.

But how do you find the *right* stimulus?

This may seem like a daunting task given how much information comes into the human machine at every moment, both in imaginary circumstances and in real life, but you're about to receive a short and simple technique that works every time.

And in order to do that, we have to move into dangerous waters. We need to engage with the actor's worst enemy, but also her best friend—the script.

KEY POINTS

1. The unconscious mind takes in stimulus, decides what's important and responds to it.

2. Humans are continually completing patterns unconsciously.

3. You can choose to direct your focus.

4. Your focus will determine your behavior.

Chapter 4

AN ORGANIC DISCOVERY PROCESS

Let's recap.

- The actor's job is to create behavior.
- Behavior is the natural response to stimulus.
- Stimulus comes to us through our senses.
- Our minds are capable of directing our attention to the most important matter at hand, whether automatically (unconsciously), or by choice (consciously).

As an actor...

How do we use information about the inner workings of our minds?

How does the Actor's Blueprint help us to live truthfully in imaginary circumstances?

And how are we going to allow authentic organic behavior to flow throughout our performance?

In this chapter, you'll learn to identify the most important behavior-generating information in the script. And, you'll learn how to use that information during the discovery process in order to engage your natural behavior-producing processes. In this way you will actually *experience* the journey of the character firsthand.

Where do you find the most important behavior-generating information in the script?

Let me first tell you where you won't find it:

It's not the dialogue.

The Problem with the Written Word

I would be remiss if I didn't tenaciously expose the dangers of dialogue right now. Dialogue, and the actor's love affair with it, is without a doubt the most crippling and debilitating monkey wrench in the actor's journey to greatness.

Like moths to a light, young actors focus almost entirely on their lines. Almost every young actor stifles his or her performance by approaching the process with the faulty internal question, "How do I say this line?"

From my experience as a teacher, I can tell you it is common for young actors to begin their scenes by speaking their lines during the rehearsal process. For the non-actor, that may sound logical, but for actors who have even just a bit of training, we quickly learn that the scene begins when the scene begins, which has nothing to do with dialogue.

Depending on the scene, there are likely several actions and/or interactions that take place before any words are spoken. Yet, it is very common for beginning actors to start verbalizing right away whilst their eyes are still in the script. They focus almost entirely on their lines because they believe that's where the most important information is. They ignore the most important part of the script, which is the context in which the words are spoken.

Beginning a scene by merely speaking is a perfect example of how actors left to their own devices give words way too much importance. *Believing that the words will lead you to a great performance is a crippling misconception.* By avoiding this misconception right now, you will jumpstart your journey toward great acting.

This is relevant to actors of all skill levels, whether they know it or not. Early in their training, many actors unknowingly focused mostly on the dialogue. This focus became habitual. It became an unconscious step in the actor's process. The scientific term for *how* we do something is called a *strategy*. Focusing primarily on dialogue becomes an inefficient step in most actors' strategies.

Identifying strategies is one of the most valuable tools in actor's training because it allows us to change our results. By observing how something is done successfully, we can simply reproduce a working strategy.

This is called *modeling* and is an important concept in the field of Neuro Linguistic Programming, the study of how language affects behavior. If we *model* successful strategies, we will produce successful outcomes.

To learn to hit a baseball, we model the perfect stance and swing. To learn to cook, we model the steps of our cooking instructor. What we seldom consider is we can also model the inner workings of our minds. And *how* we think about something, or *how* we approach a task is the most critical determinant of any outcome.

If you're a beginning actor, you may not have had the experience described in this paragraph—yet. Learn from it as you read.

If you're a seasoned or intermediate actor, chances are at some point early in your training, an instructor told you to get your face out of the script. You were directed to look at your scene partner in order to communicate with them. You learned something. You experienced what it felt like to *communicate* through the dialogue as opposed to reciting words. You continued to get positive results by implementing the strategy of looking at your partner before you spoke, and this strategy became a habit. Further down the road to acting competency, you learned to personally connect with the dialogue. This gave you good results, so you implemented a strategy of personalizing and connecting to the dialogue. For most actors these strategies were discovered outside of their awareness, or unconsciously.

Over time, given enough opportunity and experience, good actors learn to dissolve the dialogue issue through trial and error. The great actors eliminate the idea that dialogue is the driving force of their performance, and instead develop and adopt a set of strategies that create an organic process of their own.

Because most actors and acting trainers are unaware of strategies, an actor's learning curve is prolonged. In typical acting classes, instructors give feedback to actors based on the observation of individual performances. But without identifying the actor's strategy (*how* they do it), the instructor can often give positive feedback for a performance that only appears truthful. That positive feedback will reinforce a problematic strategy.

For a good portion of their careers, most actors will engage in a set of strategies to create performances that appear to be truthful, but are not organic. This type of performance will get an actor by, but it lacks authenticity. Actors can make most of their performances look just fine, but until they internalize a truly organic set of strategies, the depth and nuances of an organic experience will be missing for actor and audience alike.

You must become aware of your inefficient strategies and consciously change them, or it will take a long, long time to overcome those bad habits.

Most actors never do.

The easiest way to tell if an actor's strategy starts with the dialogue is to watch their eyes. If the mouth begins to move even a microsecond before the eyes come up, it's likely the actor's performance strategy starts with the dialogue.

Another way to spot this faulty strategy is to catch the actor consistently initiating a behavioral change, known as a beat change, right after looking at the script. These are both telltale signs the actor is allowing the dialogue to be his primary stimulus.

In the past, when acting instructors identified a student who was heavily relying on the dialogue, it wasn't likely the instructor had a *direct* and efficient manner in which to correct it.

Let's say you're an actor who recognizes you need to solve this common problem. As your instructor, I tell you to stop doing it. I tell you to look at your scene partner before you speak your dialogue. But simply looking at your partner is not a successful strategy in and of itself. Unless I can give you a concrete working strategy to replace the faulty one, it's up to you to find a working strategy all by yourself.

So how do we fix this particular faulty strategy of focusing primarily on the dialogue? We place our focus somewhere else.

It's time for a mindset shift. Let's remove the faulty assumption that dialogue is of primary importance to an actor. Change your belief system right now! Pledge now to forget "delivering the lines a certain way."

Instead, pledge to yourself, "My goal is to master my own process that produces authentic behavior in performance,"

This is the biggest mindset shift you can make to accelerate your journey to becoming a truly great actor.

Here's one last word about the words. Speaking, or verbal expression, is only one way we express ourselves. And the words we speak are actually the smallest piece of the pie in the communication model.

Linguists tell us that only 7% of communication is done with actual words. Tonal variety, pitch, tone, etc., accounts for 38% of the message sent. And 55% is physiological, such as movements, which can be gestures or facial expressions.

When a young actor poses the question, "How do I say this line?" not only are they working in a linear, non-organic and therefore non-realistic manner, they are attempting to put together a puzzle with a bunch of missing pieces.

Now we're going to install a successful strategy. We're going to shift the focus from, "How do I say this line?" to, "*What happened* that compelled me to respond using words?"

Elements of Drama

To discover *what happened*, the actor needs to identify the most important information in the script. This information is neatly packaged in the three essential *Elements of Drama*.

The three Elements of Drama essential to storytelling are:

1. Environment
2. Relationship
3. Mood

Amazingly the elements of drama also correspond with psychologists' accounts of the components that determine human behavior. Psychologists use different terms, but they directly correlate or fall within the boundaries of one of the three essential elements of drama. The three elements of drama create circumstance.

> The largest determinant of human behavior is circumstance.

"What?" the young idealist may indignantly retort. "My behavior is the result of who I am!"

To which I reply, "You are indeed unique—just like everyone else."

To understand how influential circumstance is to human behavior, let's consider John Bargh's priming experiments. Priming conveys an unconscious message to change people's behavior and is a subject of many experiments by behavioral scientists of all types. There is a wonderful explanation of Bargh's priming experiments in Malcolm Gladwell's fantastic book, blink (2005. p. 53). Gladwell describes how Bargh and his team conducted a priming experiment using subjects who take a word test. Secretly embedded in the word test are a multitude of terms that describe aging. What researchers documented is that people exit the test much slower than when they entered! There are numerous experiments and massive evidence to support that priming consistently changes human behavior.

But what I'd like to point out to actors that want to master their craft is *personalities* or *character* are not prescreened in those experiments.

Across the entire spectrum of experimentation, all ages, social statuses, races, genders, etc., have participated in these priming experiments. Researchers find consistent resulting behaviors in response to the primers. Humans behave differently when a factor in the circumstances change. In fact, humans are so sensitive to changes in the environment that behaviors change even when we are unaware of the existence of the changed stimulus. In other words, even factors of the circumstances we don't consciously recognize change our behavior.

Once again, human behavior is largely determined by circumstance, not by character.

Actors will learn much more about creating authentic behavior by focusing on the imaginary circumstances. And that's why we focus on the circumstances so meticulously in this approach.

Just because our behavior is consistent, it doesn't mean we should feel like a sheep. Let me assure you, you are still special. Although you too would leave the test a little slower than you entered it, *the way you would exit* is what makes you unique.

The exciting part of this equation is that your unique behaviors happen naturally, so we don't have to think about them. In fact, it serves your acting technique far better if you don't think about them. So forget them and focus on exploring the circumstances.

Exploring the circumstances is crucial in order to create authentic, meaning contextually accurate, behavior, and the best way to do that is to focus on the three elements of drama.

From feature film scripts, to thirty-second improvisational scenes, to stage plays, the dramatic structure must include these three elements in order for the audience to grasp the idea of a story.

- The audience must know the *environment*, or where the action is taking place.
- They must understand the *relationship* of the characters or character.
- They must understand the emotional state or *mood* of the character.

Environment + Relationship + Mood = Circumstance

Circumstances + Conflict = Story

If that simplistic formula stirs skepticism in you, try it. Let's write a scene right now. You do one scene and I'll do my own with you. Answer the first thing that comes to your mind and fill in the blanks.

Environment? Where does your scene take place?

Mine: A waterpark

Yours: _____?

Relationship?

Mine: My child

Yours: _____?

Mood? What is the mood at the top of the scene?

Mine: Aggravated at long lines

Yours: _____?

Now, just add a conflict between you and the other character or a conflict with yourself, or a conflict that makes sense in your context, and you've got a workable scene.

Here's my scene.

David is a 47-year-old father attempting to balance a career with raising children. He is on a family excursion to a water park, even though he has a looming deadline for a book he's writing. David and his two children have just come off a ride.

David: Are you guys hungry?

Kaylee: Let's go again, Dad.

David: Honey, it's gonna take us twenty minutes to get up there again.

Kaylee: Come on, Dad.

David: Fine. You two go. Last ride and then we have to leave.

Kaylee: Daaad. Whyyyy? That's not fair.

David: (losing his patience) Just go!

There you go. I just created a masterpiece in less than two minutes. Well, if not a masterpiece, at least it's a playable scene that might work in a coming-of-age story about a family drifting apart. And regardless of my writing abilities, the scene came together quickly and simply by identifying the three elements of drama, adding a conflict, and allowing my unconscious mind to easily fill in the details. Most likely you were able to do the same. We could do this exercise one hundred more times and come up with one hundred more playable scenes.

Turns out, actors are awesome story creators. I've used this formula countless times with students.

Actors come up with incredible slices of stories using this simple formula. In my classes, I've been moved to tears and had many laughs as a result of actors answering those three questions and creating scenes.

If we can use the elements of drama to construct a scene, we can also use them to deconstruct a scene.

This is why they are so valuable. They exist in every script you'll ever read and they will provide you with everything you need to create a brilliant performance.

All the important information you'll need to feed your behavior-producing machine, otherwise known as your unconscious mind, will be found in the environment, relationship and mood.

Let's briefly explore how each element affects behavior.

Environment

Environment is a massive determinant of behavior. Consider how people behave while attending a classical concert vs. a sporting event? How does behavior change between sitting in a spa vs. trekking through a frozen tundra? Upscale restaurant vs. McDonalds? Classroom vs. locker room showers? Our behaviors are largely regulated by the environment.

Relationship

Do you behave differently with your friends than you do with your religious leader? Your parents vs. your lover? How might you behave when you're alone vs. when you are meeting someone new?

Mood

Our emotional state is omnipresent and affects every moment of our lives. Imagine two scenes about an interview. Same environment, same relationship to the interviewer, but in the first scene you enter the office in a good mood, and in the second scene you enter in a bad mood. The interactions will be different. The scene will be different.

At this point in our exploration of this approach, having the following mindset about your emotional life is very beneficial: think of your emotions literally, as a bio-chemical *response* that happens automatically. Think of your emotional life as being constantly dynamic. The etymology of the word, "e-motion" actually means *out of movement*. For our purposes now, it's beneficial to think of your emotions simply as a part of your natural processes. So, identify your character's mood at the beginning of the scene as a point of departure, then forget about it and allow your natural processes to take over.

Using the Mind's Eye to "Read" a Script

Now that we know we're looking for information about the three elements of drama, let's try out a new script-reading strategy.

Read the script with your mind's eye, looking specifically to identify and consider the environment, your relationships in the scene, and your mood at the beginning of the scene. Any clues are helpful. You can and should liberally add and remove the components of the imaginary world as it suits you.

This is fun. You get to build a world in your mind. Play in your character's space. Be warned—this is a dynamic process so don't fall in love with anything just yet. The name of the game right now is volume. The more detail you imagine in your character's world, the greater the potential for organic responses and the resulting meaningful and nuanced behavior.

Let's play in the world of Hedda Gabbler.

In the first scene of Ibsen's play, *Hedda Gabbler*, the new maid, Berte and her previous employer, Aunt Juliane, are arriving to meet Hedda who they haven't seen in a long while. Hedda had arrived late the night before and is still sleeping. The new maid holds flowers in her hand and can't find a place to put them because Hedda's belongings are strewn about.

Allow me to guide your minds' eye through the world of the new maid. The play's stage directions tell you to creep in behind your previous employer as she carefully peeks inside the door.

What are you noticing? Are you craning to see around the woman obstructing your view, but her big bonnet is in the way? Are you listening for movement inside since you can't see around the other woman? Are you worried you might crush the flowers in your hands? Are you hoping Hedda is still asleep so you won't have to start working right away?

I couldn't put these down as fast as I could think of them, but all these potential stimuli came quickly as a result of imagining the character's circumstances. If you're not used to working this way, this process could potentially seem overwhelming or mysterious, and you might have missed the simple pattern, which I will point out to you shortly. But what's important is that all of those ideas came from the circumstances, and each of those ideas generates an authentic behavior for this scene.

It's time to learn how to craft your performance organically by engaging your natural behavior-producing processes in order to experience the journey of the character.

Forms of Stimulus

Remember again that behavior naturally happens as a response to stimulus, and stimulus comes to us through our senses. The first three forms of stimulus are self-explanatory:

- We see
- We hear
- We feel

Another way we receive information is *we say things to ourselves*. This is the fourth type of stimulus. "Saying things to ourselves" is as important to our acting as the other three sources of information. Scientists call our internal dialogue Auditory Digital, which loosely means self-talk.

Self-talk happens in differing degrees for all of us. And although it can likely be words, it can also be thoughts that are not words. It could be a visual memory; it could even be a gut feeling in relation to a past experience. What distinguishes self-talk is that it happens from the inside. This is one of those concepts you simply accept without expectations. However your self-talk naturally manifests itself for you is perfect. Become aware of it, and it will be a very powerful tool in your actor's toolbox.

Stimulus Key:

👁 - what you see
𝒟 - what you hear
❤ - what you feel
● - what you say to yourself

The four sources of stimulus are the key to authentic behavior. The actor who learns to explore the character's circumstances using the four sources of stimulus quickly and easily discovers incredibly accurate and useful information. In any given moment, ask yourself where your character's attention might be. Memorize this simple question: What is it that my character sees, hears, feels or says to himself, to make him respond in any given moment?

The four sources of stimulus are very powerful and effective for actors for one main reason. When an actor places their focus on something they see, something they hear, something they feel, or something they say to themselves, they automatically have a reaction. The actor does not have to think about what the reaction is, it just happens. It eliminates an actor's ability to edit herself. An actor bypasses the intellectual interruptions because there is nothing 'to think about.' Focusing on the stimulus allows the actor to exchange an artificial process (of let's say exploring a character's psychological motivation) for a natural one or an intellectual process for a visceral one.

The results speak for themselves. I have witnessed inexperienced actors create wonderfully rich and genuine behaviors by using this technique.

The upside of this approach is you will never run out of potential ideas because there are literally millions of them in each scene. This is clearly overwhelming. However, in the next chapter we will learn how to identify the relevant stimulus that will allow you to explore your character's experience in every story.

KEY POINTS

1. Read the script using your mind's eye to discover the circumstances of the story.

2. The four sources of stimulus are what we see, hear, feel and say to ourselves.

Chapter 5

DIRECTED FOCUS

Our goal is to live the life of the character. To do this, we discover the stimuli to which the character responds, and subsequently allow ourselves to naturally respond to those stimuli as they occur.

In other words, for the time being, we won't concern ourselves with the character's actual responses or behaviors, we just want to find out *what it is* that causes them to react.

We will discover what our character is responding to by exploring the three elements of drama: Environment, Relationship and Mood. We will look for the stimulus within each of the elements of drama that makes our character respond.

In any given moment of any given scene, you can ask yourself, "What is catching my character's attention at the moment? Is it something from the environment, relationship or mood?" And then decide which form of stimulus to focus on. "Is it something I see, something I hear, something I feel, or something I say to myself?" (see figure 1.2)

DIRECTED FOCUS

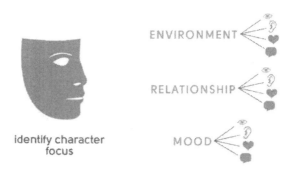

identify character
focus

figure 1.2

This is called *Directed Focus,* and as you'll see shortly, you can use it to craft an entire performance.

Directed Focus can be a conscious manipulation of an unconscious process. We naturally shift our focus to different stimulus in real life. We stare at an object to consider it. We hear the garage door open. We get excited about someone coming home. We suddenly remind ourselves about something we were supposed to do before that person came home.

Our focus can also shift naturally from real life to our imagination. Something outside of your awareness may unconsciously trigger the memory of the time your big brother dared you to bite into a lemon. Or you could consciously decide to imagine the details of biting into a lemon right now. Either way, your mouth will most likely salivate.

Directing your focus is a perfectly natural and organic process. And, lucky for the actor, the resulting behavior of directing your focus to a lemon is the same whether in real life or in your imagination.

Remember the Hedda Gabler scene?

I referred to a simple pattern you may have missed. Here is the list again, but this time the source of the information is included. You will notice each choice is one of the four sources of stimulus.

The play's stage directions tell you to creep in behind your previous employer who carefully peeks inside the door. What are you noticing?

1) *Is it something you see?* Are you craning to see around the woman obstructing your view, but her big bonnet is in the way?

2) *Is it something you hear?* Are you listening for movement inside since you can't see around the other woman?

3) *Is it something you feel?* Are you worried you might crush the flowers in your hands?

4) *Is it something you say to yourself?* Are you hoping Hedda's still asleep so you won't have to start working right away?

Do you see the beauty of this?

This is not a random list created by an acting teacher who came up with an index system with a cute acronym. The list of stimuli is used by behavioral scientists to notate the natural organic processes of human behavior. We are modeling human behavior as it organically occurs. We are literally living truthfully in imaginary circumstances the same way we live truthfully in real life.

And as you reinforce this process by repetition, it will become second nature. Over time, you won't have to think about it anymore. Your mind will begin to habitually scour the script, and your imagination will provide meaningful stimulus automatically. You will have trained yourself to use your natural processes as your acting technique.

You will be "preparing *un*consciously to perform *un*consciously."

So far, we have learned how to prepare our scenes in a way that produces authentic unconscious behaviors. Performing unconsciously will be the subject of the next chapter, but before we move on I need to answer an important question.

Exactly how often should an actor switch to a new Directed Focus?

The answer is, anytime a change in behavior happens in the scene. And that is called a beat change.

Beat Changes

A beat change, as defined in the Ihrig Approach and most other places, is a change in behavior as the result of a change in the scene. There are no right or wrong choices when it comes to beat changes. Most of the time, a beat change will choose you. It will just feel right. You'll intuitively know when something changes. However, you can also consciously make a choice to change your behaviors at a specific moment in the scene. Very often, you'll be directed to do so.

To clarify beat changes and how they work, let's take a look at the following short scene as an example of how an actor could use beat changes. Read the scene once to become familiar with it.

Laurie has been searching for John, a loved one who's gone missing. Playing a hunch, Laurie decides to search a particular campground. She discovers John who is apparently living in a tent.

Scene: It's early evening. Laurie comes upon the campsite for which she's been searching. It's inhabited.

Laurie: John? Is that you?

John: Laurie? How did you find me?

Laurie: John, I've been so worried about you... we all have.

Now read the scene again. Inserted are notations as examples of where an actor playing Laurie might insert her beat changes.

Scene: It's early evening. Laurie comes upon the campsite for which she's been searching. It's inhabited.

Laurie: (Beat Change #1 - *Laurie changes from nervous to hopeful when she recognizes John's tent.*) John? (Beat Change #2 - *Laurie changes from hopeful to cautious when he doesn't immediately answer her.*) Is that you?

John: Laurie? How did you find me? (Beat Change #3 – *Laurie changes from cautious to relieved when she sees him.*)

Laurie: John, (Beat Change #4 – *Laurie changes from relieved to affectionate.*) I've been so worried about you (Beat Change #5 - *Laurie changes from affectionate to embarrassed when she notices herself gushing over him.*)... we all have.

Beat changes can happen at any time. They can happen in the middle of your dialogue. They can happen in the middle of your scene partner's dialogue. There are often several beat changes that occur with no dialogue. And there can just as well be an entire two minute monologue, which is all one beat.

Beat changes can be pre-determined, but they can also happen organically in the moment.

Earlier, you learned you should re-direct your focus anytime there is a change in behavior, otherwise known as a beat change. And you already know that in order to re-direct your focus, you're going to search for the stimulus that caused the change in behavior. Let's put the whole thing together now and run through an example of the approach as seen through the eyes of two young actors being exposed to Directed Focus for the first time. We are going to use the Laurie and John scene.

The two young actors perform the scene with no instruction. Both novice actors make sense of this scene. But the acting is predictable and filled with general, uninteresting behavior.

After their performance, I ask the actor *why she says her first line.* She stops to think about it and clearly doesn't know. She nervously exclaims she wants to make sure she has in fact found John, which is a great answer. I ask her to identify what it is *she's specifically responding to* when she speaks her first line. Silence.

So I ask the young actor to direct her focus to an element in the scene. I tell her it can be from the environment, her relationship, or her emotional state in the scene. And she must decide whether it's something she sees, hears, feels, or says to herself. I give her a few examples of her options.

It could be something from the environment. Maybe it's an unexpected sound that freezes you because you're uncomfortable in the woods. Then your verbal expression,

"John, is that you?" could be the result of you ascertaining your safety and looking to John to provide it.

The stimulus could be from your emotional state. Maybe you're really nervous and tentative to see who is in the tent before they see you. You might be encroaching on someone else's privacy. "John, is that you?" might carry tones of uncertainty and might be apologetic in case it was someone else.

The stimulus could come out of your relationship. Maybe your sole focus is on how John will react when he sees you, and nothing else matters. Now, "John, is that you?" might be colored with love and hope.

All three of those different behaviors come out of a truthful exploration of your imaginary circumstances. All three serve the purpose of the story. All three are filled with specific behaviors that create meaning for an audience.

So, I ask her again, "What is it you notice that makes you want to make sure you have found John? Is it something in the environment, relationship, or mood?"

She replies, "Um, it's a mood or feeling. I'm scared he's gonna be sickly."

I ask her exactly when she notices that feeling and she tells me it just comes to her right after she says his name the first time. I say, "Wonderful." We work with her experience of that particular emotion for a moment, and then run the scene two more times.

The last time she performs it, she calls his name, "John?" and as he turns to her, her nose involuntarily wrinkles as if preparing for the worst. "Is that you?" Their eyes meet, and she exhales a quick little sigh of relief. Those little knee-jerk expressions were so quick, she didn't know she did them. That moment brought a beautiful truth to the scene. And it wasn't discovered by an intellectual analysis, or talked to death. It was a truthful unconscious reaction she found by simply focusing on a stimulus in the character's circumstances.

It's time for you to try out these concepts. You are going to craft an imaginary performance using Directed Focus. When you read the script for yourself, fully develop the three essential elements of drama in your mind's eye.

Imagine the environment. Notice all the details you can. If you are playing Laurie, you know you are looking for a tent, right? So use your imagination to really flesh out the space for yourself. Are there other campers close by or are you in a more secluded area? If you're playing John, what are you doing inside your tent, and how many amenities do you have? Notice your mood, or emotional state at the beginning of the scene. And create a relationship for yourself with the other character.

You can imagine the world by looking down on it from above or walking or floating around in it. However you imagine the world is fine. But once you have fully created the world of the story in your imagination, inhabit the character as yourself. When you're ready to begin the scene, you should be looking through the eyes of your character. What's the first thing you notice in that world? Is it something you see, hear, feel, or say to yourself? That's where your scene starts.

What happens next? What do you notice next? Continue to notice things in the imaginary circumstances that you see, hear, feel and say to yourself about the environment, relationship and the mood.

If you're playing Laurie, what specifically happens that makes you say your first line?

If you're playing John, what was it you noticed when she called to you? It could be you heard someone step on a stick before you heard her voice (environment—sound), and that hearing her voice confirmed someone is outside your tent. Or maybe you think you're hearing things when she calls you, which makes you really miss her (self-talk—feeling). Allow whatever your imagination gives you to play on you. Remember, there are no mistakes. Whatever you come up with is perfect.

Ready? Here's the scene again if you need the text. Begin your experience when you're ready.

Scene: It's early evening. Laurie comes upon the campsite for which she's been searching. It's inhabited.

Laurie: John? Is that you?

John: Laurie? How did you find me?

Laurie: John, I've been so worried about you... we all have.

Now, as an exercise, choose a different stimulus for the beginning of the scene, and play it out in your imagination. Do it now.

Was your experience changed a bit? Choose a different focus yet again and indulge me for one last time. Play the third one out now.

Did you do it? Because if you did, you are now thinking like a great actor!

What did you learn by doing the same scene three times using The Ihrig Approach?

What most students learn from that exercise is that their imagination can easily provide three different experiences with minimal effort. Giving their imagination the simple framework of the four sources of stimulus with the three elements of drama allows the imagination to create prolifically. And each of those experiences serve the story because they came from the story.

If you step back now for a moment, you'll notice you are allowing yourself to experience the world of the story the same way you experience reality.

Most acting techniques teach actors to make choices about the script. But in real life, we don't "choose actions" to play during our conversations. We don't imagine ourselves talking to someone "as if" we were someone else. In real life, our behavior is authentic because we simply listen during a conversation and things happen that make us respond.

Sometimes we are aware of our responses and sometimes we aren't.

As one last point, it's also worth noting that in real life, we use language to derive meaning from stimuli. Not the other way around. This approach mimics real life processes in every way.

Think about what we are doing in this approach.

By putting the stimuli first and then reacting to it, we are actively constructing life. We are actively making sense of the world created by the playwright by using the text to provide the clues.

By using Directed Focus to discover the stimulus in a scene, we are allowing our natural behavioral processes to kick-in without thinking about it. And over time, as you develop the skill of exploring the character's world in this manner, it will become second nature. That's when you will be preparing unconsciously to perform unconsciously. And you will have become a master of acting.

KEY POINTS

1. The three elements of drama are environment, relationship and mood.

2. Directed Focus mirrors our real life mental processes.

Chapter 6

THE MASTER ACTOR'S MINDSET

How do we "live truthfully?"

We notice things. And then we make sense of them.

Another way to describe the process of our existence is to say we actively construct life.

This is what we do in real life. It's what we do from the moment of conception. We construct life. We complete patterns and then store those patterns so we can build more patterns. We are constantly learning.

Observe! Draw conclusion! Store for later! Observe! Draw conclusion! Store for later! And on and on...

At one point we were children crawling across the floor in our jammies, put our hand on a round object, and it moved away from us. So, we caught up with it and put our hand on it again, and it moved away from us a second time. This was great! This round object has behaved in a predictable manner. Aha, a pattern! I will remember this. But what's this? Here is another object approximately the same size, but it's square. When I push this, it behaves differently. Hmm... that's a new pattern.

Later, language enters the equation. Mommy tells me this round thing that I roll back and forth with her on the floor is a ball. Ball. Got it. But Daddy is throwing this oblong object in the air. He also calls this a ball. And so the child deduces there is a soccer ball, and a football. But wait, there's more. There's a new thing Daddy calls a golf ball. When I see this very small, round dimpled object that is harder than the others, I know it is a ball of some sort. It's a different size and shape, and is used differently, yet I have generalized that a round thing that is used for play is in fact a ball.

The unconscious processes that scientists refer to as generalizing, distorting, and deleting describe how humans construct life. I bring them up partly for fun, and partly to point out the way the scientists describe our constant processing. We are constantly constructing life. This is how we perceive our world and interact with it. We are constantly making sense of our world. This is the core of how we "live truthfully moment to moment."

Making sense of our world is the overriding *objective* of human life.

Traditional Objectives in Acting

In acting, most teachers use the term *objective* to describe what an actor wants in a scene or a story. For example, in the scene from Hedda Gabler, the new maid Berte's objective might be to get Hedda to like her. In our example scene about Laurie and John at the campsite, Laurie's objective might be to get John to leave with her.

Actors can also choose an objective for the story. Indiana Jones wants to find the Ark of the Covenant. In Tennessee Williams' play *Cat on a Hot Tin Roof*, Maggie wants Brick to give her a child.

Traditionally, an objective is what the character wants.

Almost every traditional acting technique teaches the actor to choose an objective for each scene. Once the actor identifies the objective, he then breaks the scene into beats. The actor then assigns an *action* to play on each beat. These are sometimes labeled "tactics." An example of this sort of analytical breakdown might look something like this for the character of Laurie.

Laurie Beat 1 – Laurie beckons John.

Laurie Beat 2 – Laurie assures John.

Scene: It's early evening. Laurie comes upon the campsite for which she's been searching. It's inhabited.

Laurie: (Beat 1) John? Is that you?

John: Laurie? How did you find me?

Laurie: (Beat 2) John, I've been so worried about you... we all have.

What is the actor taught to do?

The actor is taught to identify and label the unconscious exchange of behaviors in a scene. In real life, we don't consciously decide to 'beckon' someone. Choosing an objective, assigning beats and playing actions is an artificial process. It's also decidedly an intellectual one.

What's good about choosing objectives and beats is actors *can* play actions. Playing an action is a tangible concept for virtually every actor. When I ask actors to "beckon" their scene partner, they typically have instant success in terms of tapping into something that feels like and looks like real life.

From a neurological and physiological standpoint, our brains are heavily wired for movement and action. In that way, playing actions does tap into some of the natural processes of our behavior-producing mechanisms.

And, working in this manner eventually can create an organic performance through the repetition of playing actions. As stated earlier, once you've done a thing enough times you no longer need to think about it; it becomes automatic, or unconscious.

This is why playing actions works.

I don't want to give the impression I am against the traditional method of analyzing a script. I'll say it again: every actor should use what works for him or her. What I'm proposing throughout this book is simply another option.

I will point out that using script analysis and action playing as a primary or exclusive approach creates a strategy that is artificial by nature. On the other hand, playing an action to solidify or intensify a response you have organically discovered is a great way to apply the technique.

The Objective of The Ihrig Approach

I'd like you to consider thinking of an objective in an entirely different manner. What if instead of choosing an objective for our scenes, or our stories, we choose an objective for the acting process?

I'd like actors to consider choosing just one objective for all their performances. The actor's objective should be to actively make sense of the world of the character. The actor's objective is always to *construct life*.

I'm wondering what would happen if an actor redefined the execution of the craft of acting as constructing life?

It might just create the perfect mindset to excel at the craft.

How might this work in performance?

The real question is how could it not? It works because you are unconsciously constructing life right now. So is every other living being on the planet. And so do all the characters ever written. Richard the III, and Mavis from Sign in Sidney Brustein's *Window*, and Luke Skywalker are all making sense of their worlds. The actor's job is really to construct the life of the character they are playing.

Characters are presented with problems that throw their world out of balance, and they spend the rest of the story trying to get things back in order, whatever that means to them.

In the previous chapter, we used Directed Focus during the discovery process to explore the character's experience. We identified the beats of the scene by looking for each new thing our character responded to that created a new behavior. Then we remembered those things that worked, and continued to explore to find things we liked better. We basically explored, discovered and then cataloged our character's experience so that we could live it.

I know this approach is very different from what most actors are taught. For the benefit of those who are reading this for the first time and haven't tried it yet, I want to point out something I've noticed in the studio: actors rarely "forget" what they choose to respond to.

Inexperienced actors usually marvel at the ability to memorize large chunks of text. As they become more experienced, they learn that memorizing lines can be difficult when they are simply attempting to memorize for the sake of memorization. Most of us, however, find that when we "do" the lines several times in a row, they just start coming to us.

Now that you have a better understanding of how your inner mind works, you'll realize right away that memorizing lines is an unnatural, intellectual process, but "remembering" actions to play, or in this approach, remembering what you are responding to for each beat change is easy.

Why?

Because our mechanisms are being used exactly the way they are meant to be.

In 2009, Stuart Jeffries wrote Inside the Mind of an Actor, an article that appeared in the November 23 edition of a British Newspaper called The Guardian. The article described actress Fiona Shaw's participation in an experiment held at the University of London by psychology professor Sophie Scott. Shaw had her brain scanned while alternating between reading numbers displayed on a screen in front of her and reciting text from a show she performed years earlier, which was also displayed on the screen. Researchers mapped the activity in her brain to see if there was any difference in brain activity between these two different types of speech. Not surprisingly there was. Not only did Shaw use more areas of her brain when reciting the text, but according to Scott, "used a part of the brain associated with analysing or doing a complex transformation of a visual image." Scott explained, "...that's the extra part Fiona was using when she was performing the text." Scott concluded that Shaw's results, as that of a professional actor, are different from the results of non-actors participating in the same experiment.

During an on-camera interview which can be seen on The Guardian's website, Shaw describes how information comes to her in performance. She says, "You're often in a visual architectural space in your head in order to remember it, I can't remember plays I'm in, even when I'm in them, if I'm not in a stimulused... (chooses new words) stimulated environment, I can't do it." The word "stimulused" is italicized in the quote by me in order to point out that Fiona Shaw's mind wants to use the word stimulus, which she does, but needs to change it to a descriptive word to fit into proper sentence structure, so she uses the phrase "stimulated environment." It sounds to me like Fiona Shaw's technique may be very similar to Directed Focus. She is describing how she 'remembers' using the natural mechanisms of her brain to live and re-live a performance.

For our purposes here, "remembering" can be thought of as your mind's way to store and retrieve information. Our minds evolved in this manner in order to avoid dangers like eating poison berries and walking into bear caves. Current science tells us the different pieces of information that make up a memory are stored in separate places and in different ways. Each piece is stored by a different brain mechanism, and when a relevant trigger occurs, the information is pulled together and presented to the conscious mind in the form of one cohesive memory.

For example, when a primitive human recognized the smell of a certain berry that triggered the brain mechanism that stores visual information to provide an image of her old cave-mate Boolga lying dead beside the berry bush with berry juice dripping down her chin hair.

82

The more meaningful, or in this case the more traumatic, the experience, the higher priority the memory is assigned. This is why memorizing strings of words is a difficult task that can only be accomplished by tireless repetition. But remembering a moment in Act 2 when I look to my scene partner for support, and instead catch an icy stare—that will stay with me.

This incredibly effective and sophisticated process is entirely unconscious. You really have to marvel at the machine you inhabit.

Directed Focus in Performance

Let's take a second look at Directed Focus, but this time let's explore how we might use it in performance.

In the film version of *Streetcar Named Desire*, Marlon Brando is in the middle of a scene and suddenly interrupts himself to grab a floating piece of lint out of the air. It's wonderfully engaging and a great example of unconscious performance. It's not planned, it happened because a stimulus suddenly presented itself to the actor in the moment.

What's important about this idea of using Directed Focus as a performance technique is that it happens in the moment.

If, in the moment a piece of lint flies in front of you, you grab it.

If, in the moment, your scene partner trips, you attempt to catch her.

You are simply responding in the moment within the context of your scene, or the imaginary circumstances. In a truly organic performance, if you are making sense of the world you have created, you will notice things for the first time. And because you have been practicing noticing things during the rehearsal and discovery process, those things will naturally play on you. You will have natural responses. It is that simple.

How do you get "in the moment?"

You begin to notice things. What things, you may ask? You will notice those things that help you make sense of what is happening moment by moment in the imaginary circumstances.

Remember our Hedda Gabler scene from the last chapter? Let's say you are playing the maid and the thing that worked for you was to try to listen into the next room because you couldn't see around your employer. Really listen in the moment. What's going to happen? Nobody knows. That's the wonderful part. You don't know what's going to happen any more than the character does. You *may* actually hear something. And then you may rightfully assume that Hedda is in that room waiting for you. And then you may wish to straighten yourself and prepare, and then you walk in the room... and she's not there. You look around, a bit confused, and then you hide your confusion from your previous employer, and the scene continues, moment by moment, as you notice the next thing and the next and the next, and you work to make sense of it all.

All those moments of real behavior I just described don't come from the script. They don't necessarily come from playing an action. They come from accepting the reality of the situation and noticing the things that present themselves in the moment.

If you want to be a great actor, begin noticing things in the imaginary circumstances and make sense of them as your character.

It's really not that difficult and, most importantly, there's no mystery to it.

A very experienced casting director once said to me, "The great film actors are always thinking. You can see them working to solve the problem in every scene."

I began to look for that attribute and sure enough, he was right. The people we love to watch are always thinking on camera. They are always actively solving a problem, or working to get out of a situation. I spent a lot of my young actor's time figuring out how to think on camera. And I incorrectly experimented with attempting to think the character's thoughts. It didn't work because it was an *intellectual* process.

Now that I understand what he meant by 'thinking,' I can pass this on. He meant the great film actors are always making sense of their world. They were figuring things out in the moment. This is another way of saying they were constructing life. This is the secret to compelling unconscious performance. Experience the life of the character by seeing what they see, hearing what they hear, feeling what they feel, and say to yourself what they say to themselves.

While performing, develop the habit of actively making sense of your character's world at all times. Develop the habit of noticing things in performance. Search for meaning in your character's experience and you will create spontaneous unconscious behavior.

This is the path to becoming a master actor.

KEY POINTS

1. Human development is a constant process of constructing life.

2. An actor's overall objective should be to construct the life of the character.

3. Develop the habit of noticing things so that it becomes second nature in performance.

The Ihrig Approach

What next?

Well, practice.

I truly believe actors who *practice* the techniques in this book will have significant advantages in the market place. In reality, few actors ever get past mediocrity. Out of the millions of actors that engage in the craft of acting every year, only a tiny percentage learn to create truly authentic behavior.

And if the ideas in this book appeal to you, I have good news for you; there's more. Now that you have a basic understanding of your own machinery, there is a world of possibilities open to you.

Use Directed Focus to construct the character's experience and you will lay the foundation for your own excellent technique. But, there is more to learn.

For instance, a comprehensive exploration of real human behavior needs to address *implicit memory*. Implicit memory, or the unconscious influence from past experiences, is a critical component in every character's behavior. Imagine how a systemized approach to working with a character's past experiences will deepen and enhance your performances. (This book is on its way.)

Each actor must also have a systemized way to work with his or her emotional life. Actors work with emotions in two ways. The first we talked about in this book. Emotions are one of the natural ongoing processes your acting machine uses to encode and decode experiences. Allowing this natural process to flow through performances is imperative.

Actors also sometimes need to begin a scene with a strong emotional state. Many techniques teach actors how to manufacture an emotional state. In The Ihrig Approach, we look to contemporary science and find there is an *optimal way* for actors to create emotions by using our machinery the way it is intended to be used.

In truth, there is an optimal way to carry out each task in the acting process. This is an extremely exciting prospect, and it is the mission of the Ihrig Approach to help each actor discover his or her 'optimal way' in the shortest amount of time possible.

I have adapted a tool previously used by therapists to notate the primary response systems of their patients. Therapists use it to better understand how their patients approach their problems. I use the tool to identify the primary response systems of actors. It is called the Actor's Assessment.

Since Directed Focus requires the actor to explore the scene using sensory information, it becomes advantageous for an actor to identify their dominant or primary response mode.

That is why I am offering readers of this book the free use of the Actor's Assessment. Put aside ten minutes of quiet time. Go to my website, ExcellenceInActing.com, and click on the Actor's Assessment tab. Complete the short questionnaire, and as a free gift, I will send your results identifying your personal *primary response mode* along with simple instructions so that you can employ your newfound knowledge.

Knowing your primary response mode will allow you to work more efficiently in Directed Focus. But there are other benefits, as well. Discovering how you work best will allow you to better assimilate notes from directors and casting agents, make instant acting choices during auditions, and bring an overall awareness to your personal process that few actors enjoy.

Enjoy your journey,

David

For more information, visit:

TheIhrigApproach.com

or

ExcellenceInActing.com

Or, write me at:

TheIhrigApproach@gmail.com

Bibliography

Books

"authentic." Webster's Ninth New Collegiate Dictionary. 1986. Print.

Becker, Gavin De. (1997) The Gift of Fear: Survival Signals that Protect Us from Violence. Boston: Little, Brown.

"behavior." Webster's Ninth New Collegiate Dictionary. 1986. Print.

Constantine Stanislavski. (1989) An Actor Prepares. New York: Routledge.

Gladwell, Malcom. (2005) blink; The Power of Thinking Without Thinking. New York: Little, Brown and Company.

Hill, Napoleon. (1960) Think & Grow Rich. First Fawcet Crest edn. New York: Ballantine Books.

McKee, R. (1997) Story – Substance, Structure, Style, and the Principles of Screenwriting. New York: Harpers and Collins.

Articles

Jeffries, Stuart. (2009) 'Inside the Mind of An Actor', The Guardian. November 23, 2009. Available at: http://www.theguardian.com/science/video/2009/nov/24/fiona-shaw-brain-scan (Accessed: January 2015).

Videos

Jeffries, Stuart. (2009) The Guardian. Available at: http://www.theguardian.com/science/video/2009/nov/24/fiona-shaw-brain-scan (Accessed: January 2015).

Index

INDEX

G

Gabbler, Hedda, 51

great acting, 9-10, 15, 18, 21, 27, 32, 35, 41

Group Theater, 12-13

H

Hill, Napoleon, 35

I

Ibsen, Henrik, 12

Ihrig Approach, The, 8

    objective of, 70

imaginary circumstances, 10

implicit memory, 80

L

left brain, 24

R

S

T